Made in the USA
Monee, IL
16 March 2024

55152938R00061